Reproducible R

Bullying

> **Identify**

> **Cope**

> **Prevent**

Grades 7–8

World Teachers Press®

www.worldteacherspress.com

Foreword

Bullying has been likened by some commentators to lifestyle physical ailments prevalent in modern society, such as obesity, smoking-related disease, heart disease and even skin cancers. The "likeness" is that, in a majority of cases, adequate and appropriate preventive measures will stop the condition from arising altogether. All too often, bullying is treated as a condition only after it manifests itself, rather than pre-emptively, before it actually arises.

Bullying is a complex issue. It requires an ongoing education of students to develop skills and strategies to allow them to IDENTIFY, COPE with and, ultimately, PREVENT bullying from occurring.

This series provides developmental activities to promote positive attitudes in students, forestalling the development of injurious, bullying behavior.

Titles in this series:
>   *Bullying,* Grades 3–4
>   *Bullying,* Grades 5–6
>   *Bullying,* Grades 7–8

Contents

Teacher's Notes

Each student page is supported by a teacher's page which provides the following information.

Specific **indicators** explain what the students are expected to demonstrate through completing the activities.

Teacher information provides the teacher with detailed additional information to supplement the student page.

Did You Know? is a collection of background information on bullying behavior, covering interesting statistics and informative research facts.

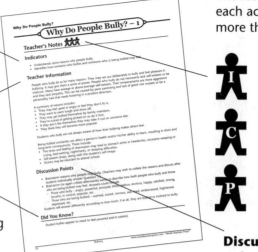

The icons below indicate the focus of each activity. Some activities may have more than one icon.

Activities to assist students to **identify** bullying behavior and why people bully.

Activities to help students **cope** with bullying behavior.

Activities where students learn strategies to **prevent** bullying behavior in themselves and/or others.

Discussion Points have been suggested to further develop ideas on the student page.

Each book is divided into four sections.

What Is Bullying? (pages 14 – 25)

The activities in this section give students opportunities to identify what bullying is and the various forms it can take.

Most definitions of bullying agree:
- It is deliberately hurtful, either physically or psychologically.
- It is repeated often over time.
- It is difficult for the person being bullied to defend himself/herself against it – he/she is weaker physically or psychologically.

Bullying can be divided into three types:
1. Physical – including hitting, punching, shoving, pinching, tripping, spitting, scratching, damaging, hiding or stealing belongings, throwing objects at someone, or locking someone in or out
2. Verbal – name-calling, making offensive remarks, taunting, teasing, put-downs
3. Emotional – spreading rumors, gossiping about or embarrassing someone, making fun of someone, using threatening looks or gestures, excluding or threatening to exclude from groups, ignoring, ostracizing or alienating

Note: In each level of *Bullying*, the word "bully" is used as a verb and not a noun. In this way, the bullying behavior is emphasized and not the child. Instead of labeling a child a "bully," he/she is referred to as "a person who bullies."

Why Do People Bully? (pages 26 – 33)

People bully for a wide variety of reasons. These include feeling they don't fit in, disliking themselves, peer pressure, wanting to show off, feeling upset or angry, or having a fear of being bullied themselves. This is not necessarily due to low self-esteem or insecurity; in fact, it can be quite the opposite. However, most people who bully have a lack of empathy, which can be caused by poor parenting, a lack of good role models or be a personality trait that needs fostering in a positive direction.

In this section, students are encouraged to explore and discuss bullying scenarios and consider possible reasons for each. Teachers will also find useful activities to help them work on anger management with students. In addition, students will learn that those who bully vary widely in physical appearance and background.

Teacher's Notes

How Does Bullying Make You Feel? (pages 34 – 41)

The activities in this section emphasize the importance of respecting the feelings and emotions of others. They require students to "put themselves in the shoes" of the person being bullied and the person who is bullying. Students are encouraged to empathize with others and to understand and deal with their own feelings. The peer group which supports and reinforces the bullying behavior is also encouraged to develop empathy for the person being bullied.

The advantages of using this approach include:
- Everyone gains a clear understanding of what bullying is.
- The focus is on finding a solution and not finding someone to blame.
- The person being bullied is able to express his or her feelings and deal with the situation.
- When people around develop empathy for the person being bullied, the dynamics of the situation change.
- Many instances of bullying rely on keeping information quiet. However, where the feelings on bullying are known to everybody it is harder for the bullying practices to continue.
- Understanding the feelings of all involved can help lay the foundations for proactive prevention of potential bullying situations.

It is recommended that a set of rules on speaking and listening be established in the classroom, with students given the chance to regularly discuss a variety of subjects so an environment exists where they feel safe to express their feelings. If such a safe environment exists, the discussion sections accompanying each activity should produce better results and maximum participation.

What Can You Do? (pp. 42 – 67)

This section of the book provides different strategies to help students cope with and prevent bullying behavior. It offers activities that promote a school ethos where bullying is openly discussed and seen as unacceptable behavior. Students are given the opportunity to discuss tolerance and friendship and to learn strategies to promote communication, problem-solving and conflict resolution. Those students who are assertive and can discuss their feelings will develop a higher self-esteem and are less likely to become victims or people who bully.

Teaching problem-solving strategies through discussion and role-playing will assist students to learn and develop skills for positive social behaviors and relationships. Beginning sentences with "I" statements, having confident body language and being assertive without becoming aggressive can be very effective ways of letting someone who is showing bullying behavior know that his/her actions will not be tolerated. Teachers can help by running drama sessions where students participate in exercises where they need to stand confidently, use eye contact and speak clearly.
Deep breathing to relax the body can also help.

Students can be taught to use other strategies to deal with bullying behavior, such as avoiding the situation whenever possible and knowing when to ask for help. Asking for help is essential, especially for victims who are not able to attempt the strategies above or for those who have tried these techniques and find they are not working. Some bullying situations can be stopped early on before the bullying cycle begins through intervention by peers, teachers, parents, or other adults.

Teacher's Notes

Working with Parents

Support from parents is vitally important to help encourage a "non-bullying" environment in the classroom or school. Parental approval is very important to students and most parents are eager to support anti-bullying programs. Parents are also often the first to detect signs that their child is being bullied or is bullying others.

Teachers can encourage parents to become involved by:
- encouraging open communication
- providing bullying information and statistics
- encouraging them to watch for signs that their child is involved in a bullying situation, and to report it as soon as possible
- taking parents' concerns about bullying seriously
- asking them to discourage their child from using bullying behavior
- giving advice on how to solve conflict without violence or aggression
- encouraging them to talk to their child about what is happening at school

Tips for Creating a Non-bullying School Environment

Much has been documented and written on the subject of bullying and findings between schools may differ. However, the approach universally agreed on is that for schools to successfully and effectively tackle the problem of bullying, a whole-school approach is needed.

Successful anti-bullying initiatives have included the following:
- Include teachers, students, administration staff, parents and even the wider community in the consultation process, and the development and implementation of policy.
- Collect information about bullying in your school and define a whole-school philosophy.
- Create a written policy document that presents a mission statement, the rights and responsibilities of students, teachers and parents, and the procedures.
- Make the policy well known.
- Ensure active supervision in the school grounds and help create situations that teach students how to play and interact together.
- Acknowledge the important role that bystanders can play in reducing bullying.
- Teach non-aggressive strategies such as problem-solving and conflict-resolution skills.
- Continually monitor and maintain the policy.
- Create team-based social relationships at the class level and encourage participation by all students. Provide opportunities for all students to get to know each other well.
- Measure social relationships between students at a class-level and be aware of potential bullying problems.
- Be aware of early warning signs.

Teacher's Notes

Explanations of the generic pages included in this book are outlined below:

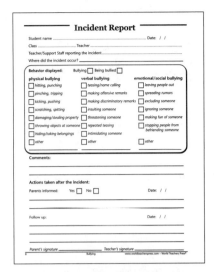

The *Incident Report* (page 8) can be used by teachers and support staff to record bullying incidents. The teacher can detail any procedures that are introduced as a result of the event and keep records of parental involvement and follow up actions.

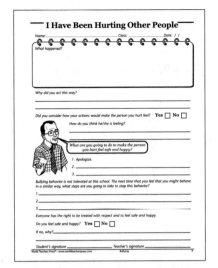

I Have Been Hurting Other People (page 9) is designed to be completed by students who have instigated or participated in bullying behavior. The student describes the incident in pictures or words and explains his or her actions. The student is asked to consider the feelings of the person(s) they have hurt. It also allows the student to assess how he or she is feeling.

I Have a Problem (page 10) is constructed for students who have experienced bullying behavior. The student explains the problem and devises steps that may help to solve it. A list of strategies is included that will assist the student in learning and developing skills for positive social behaviors and relationships.

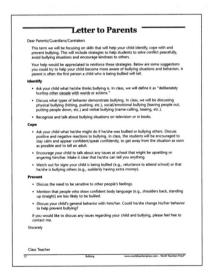

This *Questionnaire* (page 11) can be used by teachers to reveal individual or class perceptions about bullying and its existence in the school. The student is asked to consider the effects of bullying on them personally and provides the students with an opportunity to consider who is responsible for stopping bullying in their school.

A *Letter to Parents* (page 12) is provided to inform and gain the support of parents and care givers concerning bullying behavior.

Merit Certificates (page 13) are included to recognize and promote positive behavior.

Incident Report

Student Name: .... Date: / /

Class: .... Teacher: ....

Teacher/Support Staff reporting the incident: ....

Where did the incident occur? _____

Behavior displayed: Bullying ☐   Being bullied ☐

physical bullying	**verbal bullying**	**emotional/social bullying**
☐ hitting, punching	☐ teasing/name calling	☐ leaving people out
☐ pinching, tripping	☐ making offensive remarks	☐ spreading rumors
☐ kicking, pushing	☐ making discriminatory remarks	☐ excluding someone
☐ scratching, spitting	☐ insulting someone	☐ ignoring someone
☐ damaging/stealing property	☐ threatening someone	☐ making fun of someone
☐ throwing objects at someone	☐ repeated teasing	☐ stopping people from befriending someone
☐ hiding/taking belongings	☐ intimidating someone	
☐ other	☐ other	☐ other

_____   _____   _____

Comments:

_____

_____

Actions taken after the incident:

Parents informed: Yes ☐   No ☐   Date: / /

_____

_____

Follow up: Date: / /

_____

_____

_____

Parent's signature _____ *Teacher's signature* _____

I Have Been Hurting Other People

Name: .... Class: .... Date: / /

What happened?

Why did you act this way?

_____

_____

Did you consider how your actions would make the person you hurt feel? **Yes** ☐ **No** ☐

How do you think he/she is feeling?

_____

_____

What are you going to do to make the person you hurt feel safe and happy?

1. Apologize.

2. _____

3. _____

Bullying behavior is not tolerated at this school. The next time that you feel that you might behave in a similar way, what steps are you going to take to stop this behavior?

1. _____

2. _____

3. _____

Everyone has the right to be treated with respect and to feel safe and happy.

Do you feel safe and happy? **Yes** ☐ **No** ☐

If no, why? _____

_____

Student's signature _____   Teacher's signature _____

I Have a Problem

Name: .... Class: .... Date: / /

Explain your problem.

_____
_____
_____
_____
_____
_____

Who is involved?

_____
_____
_____
_____
_____
_____
_____

What would you like to happen?

_____
_____

What steps could you take to solve the problem?

1. _____
2. _____
3. _____

Will this be fair for everyone?

Yes ☐

No ☐

Check the strategies that will help you the next time you have a problem.

☐ Be assertive
☐ Avoid the situation
☐ Tell someone
☐ Use "I" statements
☐ Try to solve the conflict through peer mediation

☐ Think positive thoughts
☐ Be confident
☐ Be tolerant
☐ Take deep breaths
☐ Tell myself that I deserve to be safe and happy

Possible Solution

_____
_____
_____
_____
_____
_____
_____
_____

Student's signature _____

Teacher's signature _____

Questionnaire

School: .... Date: / /

Boy ☐   Girl ☐   Age:_____

❶ Have you ever been bullied at this school?

☐ never   ☐ a few times   ☐ about once a week   ☐ more than once a week

❷ What type of bullying?

☐ been teased   ☐ been left out   ☐ been hit, kicked, pinched, punched or shoved

☐ been called names   ☐ had my things damaged or stolen   ☐ been sworn at

☐ received a mean letter   ☐ other, such as _____

❸ Where did the bullying take place?

☐ in the classroom   ☐ on the playground   ☐ in the bathroom

☐ outside the school   ☐ other

❹ Who did you tell?

☐ teacher   ☐ friend   ☐ parent   ☐ no one   ☐ other

❺ How did you feel when you were bullied?

_____

❻ Did the bullying have any effect on you? Yes ☐   No ☐

If yes, explain. _____

❼ Have you ever seen bullying at this school?

☐ never   ☐ a few times   ☐ about once a week   ☐ more than once a week

❽ What type of bullying have you seen?

☐ teasing   ☐ being left out   ☐ hitting, kicking, pinching, punching or shoving

☐ name-calling   ☐ damaging or stealing things   ☐ swearing

☐ receiving a mean letter   ☐ other such as _____

❾ Where did the bullying take place?

☐ in the classroom   ☐ on the playground   ☐ in the bathroom

☐ outside the school   ☐ other

❿ Who did you tell?

☐ teacher   ☐ friend   ☐ parent   ☐ no one   ☐ other

⓫ Who do you think should be responsible for stopping bullying?

☐ person bullying   ☐ teachers   ☐ principal   ☐ parents of person bullying

☐ parents of victim

Letter to Parents

Dear Parents/Guardians/Caretakers,

This term we will be focusing on skills that will help your child identify, cope with and prevent bullying. This will include strategies to help students to solve conflict peacefully, avoid bullying situations and encourage kindness to others.

Your help would be appreciated to reinforce these strategies. Below are some suggestions you could try to help your child become more aware of bullying situations and behaviors. A parent is often the first person a child who is being bullied will tell.

Identify

- Ask your child what he/she thinks bullying is. In class, we will define it as "deliberately hurting other people with words or actions."

- Discuss what types of behavior demonstrate bullying. In class, we will be discussing physical bullying (hitting, pushing, etc.), social/emotional bullying (leaving people out, putting people down, etc.) and verbal bullying (name-calling, teasing, etc.).

- Recognize and talk about bullying situations on television or in books.

Cope

- Ask your child what he/she might do if he/she was bullied or bullying others. Discuss positive and negative reactions to bullying. In class, the students will be encouraged to stay calm and act and speak confidently, to get away from the situation as soon as possible and to tell an adult.

- Encourage your child to talk about any issues at school that might be upsetting or angering him/her. Make it clear that he/she can tell you anything.

- Watch out for signs your child is being bullied (e.g., reluctance to attend school) or that he/she is bullying others (e.g., suddenly having extra money).

Prevent

- Discuss the need to be sensitive to other people's feelings.

- Mention that people who show confident body language (e.g., shoulders back, standing up straight) are less likely to be bullied.

- Discuss your child's general behavior with him/her. Could he/she change his/her behavior to help prevent bullying?

If you would like to discuss any issues regarding your child and bullying, please feel free to contact me.

Sincerely,

Class Teacher

Merit Certificates

Brilliant Teamwork!

For: _____

Group name: _____

Date: _____ Signed: _____

Teacher Award
Thank You For ...

_____

_____

Name: _____

Date: _____

Signed: _____

Goal Achievement Award

Name: _____

Date: _____

Signed: _____

What is Bullying?

Teacher's Notes

Indicators

- Discusses and categorizes scenarios into those that are bullying and those that are not.
- Explains choices.

Teacher Information

Most definitions of bullying agree:
- It is deliberately hurtful (physically or psychologically).
- It is repeated over time.
- It is difficult for the person being bullied to defend himself/herself against it—he/she is weaker physically or psychologically.

People who bully use their power, physically or psychologically, to dominate, manipulate and frighten others who are less powerful than they are. It is important that every person realizes he/she has the right to feel safe.

Discussion Points

- Before handing out the worksheet, ask the class to brainstorm words and phrases that describe bullying. Collate the phrases to make a class definition. Is it similar to the one on the worksheet?
- Is calling someone a name once bullying? Why/Why not?
- Is pushing someone over at lunch time bullying? Why/Why not?
- Is taking someone's lunch money every Friday bullying? Why/Why not? Go through each of the scenarios. Tally the number of students who think it probably is or probably isn't bullying behavior. It may be interesting to witness or read the responses of the students who are more inclined to bully.

Did You Know?

One in seven children is either someone who bullies or a victim of bullying.

What is Bullying?

Bullying is usually deliberate, hurtful treatment that is repeated over time. The person bullying has more power, physically or psychologically, than the person being bullied.

Read each of the incidents and complete the form below. Decide whether or not the incident is a form of bullying and explain why or why not.

Incident	Is this a type of bullying?		Why or why not?
	probably	probably not	
1			
2			
3			
4			
5			
6			
7			
8			
9			
10			

1 Tuyen usually eats lunch alone because people often make fun of the type of food she is eating.

2 Often, Jemma makes a rude comment about what Laura is wearing, Kia laughs.

3 Talia wears leg braces to help her walk. When she first came to her new school, Tyler called her "Stumpy." Now, all the kids call her that—and she hates it.

4 Adara is new to the school. No one has asked her to play with them and some kids have made fun of her dark skin color.

5 Tom loses his temper easily. He tends to solve his arguments by punching, pushing, or kicking.

6 Jarod says to Tao, "Each day you will give me five bucks to protect you."

7 Bevan waits outside the school gate. When Aiko tries to walk past him, he won't let her and keeps blocking her path. She is forced to take the long way home.

8 Rosie asks a group of classmates playing basketball if she can join in. Anna, the most popular of the group says "No! Only people who can catch can play."

Rosie walks away.

9 Lisa is reading while she is eating lunch. Astrid walks up and snatches the book away from her. Lisa grabs it back and says, "You might want to ask first before you go taking my books."

10 Rico is walking across the playground to the classroom after lunch. Jack runs up behind him and tackles him to the ground. Jack gets up, walks off, turns, and says, "You coming or what?"

Types of Bullying

Teacher's Notes

Indicators

- Categorizes types of bullying behavior.
- Ranks bullying behavior from the most to the least serious.

Teacher Information

Bullying can be divided into the following categories:
- Physical – hitting, punching, tripping, spitting, kicking, pushing, scratching, damaging property or possessions, stealing, throwing objects at someone, performing humiliating acts on someone, hiding or taking belongings.
- Social/Emotional – Spreading rumors/nasty stories; making fun of someone; excluding from groups; ignoring, ostracizing or alienating.
- Verbal – name-calling; making offensive remarks; insulting someone, such as negative comments about a person's appearance, clothing, or actions; taunts, teasing, or threats.
- Intimidation – playing dirty tricks; defacing or taking possessions; threatening looks or gestures; intimidating or threatening phone calls, emails, messages, notes; extortion; threats of aggression against people, property, or possessions.
- Written – intimidating or harassing through emails, notes, letters, graffiti, etc.
- Discrimination – ethnic slurs, racism, slurs against children with special needs.
- Criminal – threatening with a weapon, sexual assault, physical assault, stealing property, vandalism.

Note: Criminal activity should be handled by the police or other appropriate authorities.

Discussion Points

- Discuss each of the different types of bullying. Ask the students to give simple examples of each type of bullying behavior. Stress that names are not to be used in the examples.
- Create a tally of the "seriousness rank" the students have completed on their charts. Was there a varied response?
- Identify which of the actions on the chart have been witnessed on the school grounds; in the classroom. Explain to the class that it is important that names are not used during the lesson and that times can be arranged for teacher-student conferences to discuss specific incidents.
- Whose responsibility is bullying in schools?
- Is criminal activity a matter for the schools or the police?

Did You Know?

The most common form of bullying is verbal.

Types of Bullying

1 Add four more incidents to the list and check the types of bullying they are.

2 Rank the incidents in order of seriousness from 1 to 15 (with 15 being the least serious).

Rank	Incident	Physical	Social	Verbal	Intimidation	Written	Discrimination	Criminal
	Taking someone's property							
	Hiding someone's property							
	Hitting someone							
	Spreading rumors about someone							
	Teasing someone about their appearance							
	Writing threatening graffiti about someone							
	Calling someone a name							
	Tripping someone							
	Purposely leaving someone out of a group							
	Teasing someone about their background							
	Sending a threatening text message to someone							

Bullying on Television

Teacher's Notes

Indicators

- Identifies bullying behaviors on television.
- Discusses the portrayal of bullying on television.
- Discusses the effect of bullying on television.

Teacher Information

What effect does bullying on television have on us? An association between violence on television and aggression has been well established over the last few decades. There is a need for students to develop critical viewing skills to decrease the negative effects of media violence and bullying on them. In developing these skills they learn to distance themselves from the dramatization and to recognize and understand the differences between television and real life. In this lesson, students are directed to identify bullying behaviors in programs they watch regularly. They also begin to identify and become aware of situations involving racism, violence, negative stereotypes and sexism.

They may notice a change in their reactions to the incidents once they are focusing on them. What does television tell students about bullying? What role does television play in either condoning or criticizing this behavior?

Discussion Points

- Discuss the headings on the "Bullying on Television" survey sheet so students are aware of what is expected. (Keywords and phrases can be used.)
- Students keep a tally of incidents at the bottom of the page and describe examples on the chart.
- Students could watch the same program over time to list examples accurately.
- Discuss the results. Ask students if they feel differently about the program after doing this exercise.
- Discuss the following:
  - Were any of the behaviors funny? If so, why?
  - Did anyone not think they were funny? Why not?
  - Is it possible for a sitcom or a cartoon to be funny without put-downs, etc.? How?
  - Can students think of times that they have been put-down, teased, or bullied? How did they feel?
  - Was it funny? Why or why not?
  - Is this behavior condoned? If so, how?
  - Is it criticized? How?
  - What is the program telling us about bullying?

Did You Know?

The most common form of verbal bullying is name-calling.

Bullying on Television

Program: _____ **Rating:** _____ **Time Slot:** _____

By whom	To whom	Bullying incident	Reasons for bullying	Reaction	How would you have reacted?

❷ What is one positive and one negative effect of showing bullying on television?

(a) positive _____

(b) negative _____

Stereotypes of People Who Bully

Teachers Notes

Indicator

- Describes what they think is a traditional stereotype of someone who bullies.
- Understands that a person who bullies is identified by the way he/she acts.

Teacher Information

A stereotype can be described as a very simple—and often incorrect—picture that people have of a particular type of person.

A person who bullies is traditionally thought of as someone who is bigger, stronger and shows more aggression than others. If we rely on this stereotype it could lead to students not being believed if the person who is bullying does not fit the description.

A shorter, frail-looking person can bully by name-calling, isolating others socially, teasing and using put-downs. This can be just as distressing as physical bullying.

Observations show that people who bully often, but not always, have these characteristics:
- They are generally bigger and stronger than those they bully.
- They have a strong desire to dominate.
- They are defiant and confrontational towards teachers, family members and authority figures.
- They often come from homes where problems are solved physically or in verbal arguments and have not been taught or witnessed empathy.

Whatever a person who bullies looks like, it is the physical or psychological power he/she has over the victim that identifies him/her as someone who bullies.

Discussion Points

- What does the word "stereotype" mean?
- What do you think a person who bullies looks like? How would he/she act?
- Collate the answers to Question 1 and discuss.
- Can you tell a person who bullies by what he/she looks like?
- Think of characters in television shows or movies who bully. Do any of them fit your description?
- Which are/are not stereotypes?

Did You Know?

On average, bullying episodes are usually short, lasting for about 37 seconds.

Stereotypes of People Who Bully

❶ Describe a traditional stereotype of someone who bullies. Illustrate your description.

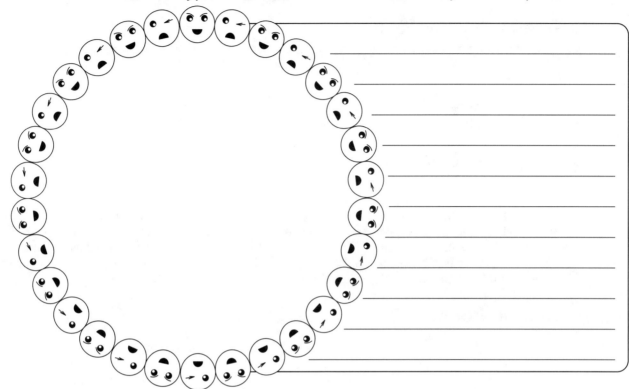

_____

_____

_____

_____

_____

_____

_____

_____

_____

_____

❷ Make a list of characters on TV or in the movies who bully others. Indicate if they are stereotypical or not.

Character	Program/Movie name	Stereotype	Not a stereotype

❸ What can happen if we rely on stereotypes to identify a person who bullies?

_____

_____

_____

_____

Bullying in the Media

Teacher's Notes

Indicators

- Locates and reads reports of bullying in the media.
- Identifies ways these reports can help solve bullying in his/her school.

Teacher Information

Students may read newspaper reports or hear television news reports containing disturbing information about bullying. These may include accounts of children (usually teenagers) committing suicide after years of constant bullying, or killings of teachers and students by victims of bullying. Be prepared to discuss these incidents tactfully and with sensitivity. Allow students to express their feelings and to focus on preventive strategies. The effects of bullying can have long-term consequences for both students who bully and for their victims, and these should not be under-emphasized.

Discussion Points

- Read the reports to the class or have individual students read each report.
- How does it make you feel when you read about these incidents?
- In any of the articles, are there any preventive measures that could have been or should have been taken?
- How can what you have read or heard about other bullying incidents help at your school?

Did You Know?

Students involved in bullying (whether bullying or being bullied) usually have poor social skills and problems at home.

Bullying in the Media

The following chart outlines some events concerning bullying, as reported in the media.

Source	Date	Statement
Time Magazine	*May 13, 2002*	*Rosalind Wiseman has written a chilling account of the life girls navigate in their school lunchrooms and hallways.* *…psychologists who study mothers and daughters suggest that mothers can be hugely influential, even after trouble starts.*
NEA Today (National Education Assoc.)	*Feb. 2002*	*Bullying in schools is much more prevalent and serious today than 15 years ago. The effects of bullying can last a lifetime for the bully and the victim. NEA's National Bullying Awareness Campaign creates an awareness of the problem of bullying.*
Knight Ridder Newspapers	*August 15, 2002*	*At a teen think tank organized through San Ramon school district and Del Valle Council of PTA's, 20 middle school students gathered to talk about why teasing and bullying happens and what can be done about it.*

❶ Write three things you learned about bullying from the information above.

❷ Discuss how articles outlining bullying events can help solve bullying problems in our own schools. Record discussion points.

_____

_____

_____

_____

_____

❸ Add two more examples of "Bullying in the Media" to the chart above.

Bullying Situations

Teacher's Notes

Indicator

- Uses role-play and discussion to solve bullying situations.

Teacher Information

Teaching problem-solving strategies through discussion and role-playing will assist students in learning and developing skills for positive social behavior relationships.

Students could role-play each of the situations in small groups, then discuss possible solutions to role-play.

Discussion Points

After students have role-played situations, discuss:
- How did you feel about the role-play?
- Was the problem solved? How was it solved? or, Why wasn't it solved?
- Should anything have been done differently?
- What did you learn?

Did You Know?

Children who bully are four times more likely than others to come before the courts and to be convicted of antisocial offenses.

Bullying Situations

❶ Role-play then write a
solution next to each of
the scenarios.

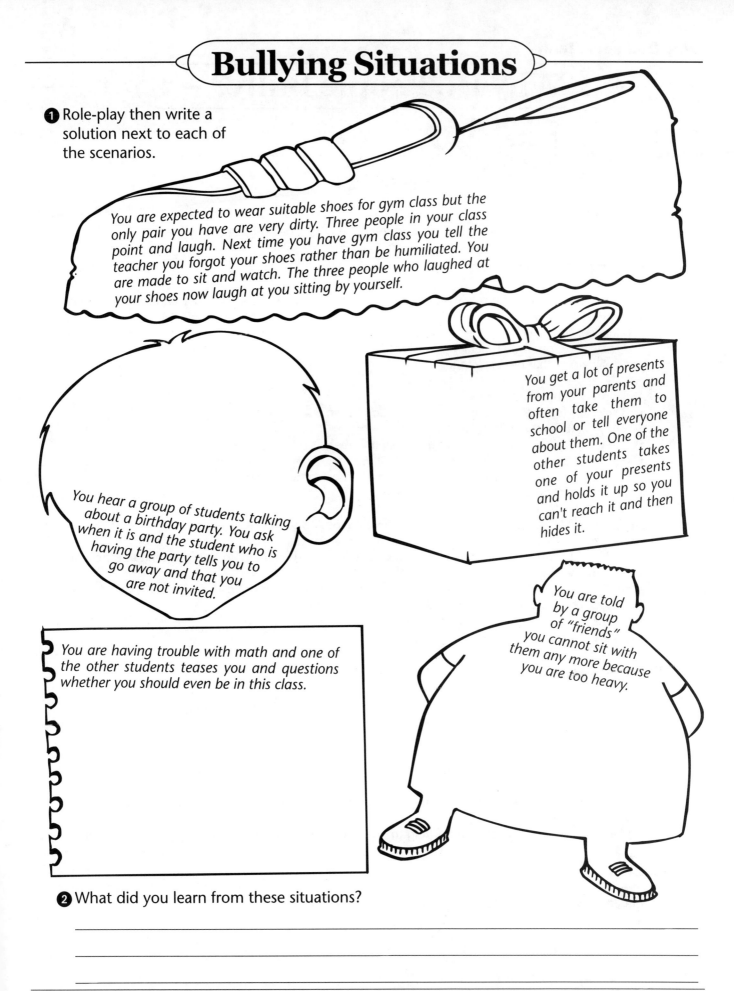

You are expected to wear suitable shoes for gym class but the only pair you have are very dirty. Three people in your class point and laugh. Next time you have gym class you tell the teacher you forgot your shoes rather than be humiliated. You are made to sit and watch. The three people who laughed at your shoes now laugh at you sitting by yourself.

You get a lot of presents from your parents and often take them to school or tell everyone about them. One of the other students takes one of your presents and holds it up so you can't reach it and then hides it.

You hear a group of students talking about a birthday party. You ask when it is and the student who is having the party tells you to go away and that you are not invited.

You are having trouble with math and one of the other students teases you and questions whether you should even be in this class.

You are told by a group of "friends" you cannot sit with them any more because you are too heavy.

❷ What did you learn from these situations?

_____

_____

_____

Why Do People Bully? – 1

Teacher's Notes

Indicators

- Understands some reasons why people bully.
- Identifies how someone who bullies and someone who is being bullied may feel.

Teacher Information

People who bully do so for many reasons. They may set out deliberately to bully and feel pleasure in bullying. It may give them a sense of power. People who bully do not necessarily lack self-esteem and confidence. Many have average or above-average self-esteem. Their temperaments are more aggressive and they lack empathy. This can be caused by poor parenting and lack of good role models or be a personality trait that needs fostering in a positive direction.

A summary of reasons includes:
- They may feel upset or angry or feel they don't fit in.
- They want to seem tough and show off.
- They may get bullied themselves by family members.
- They're scared of getting picked on so do it first.
- If they don't like themselves, they may take it out on someone else.
- They think they will become more popular.

Students who bully are not always aware of how their bullying makes others feel.

Being bullied constantly can affect a person's health and his/her ability to learn, resulting in short- and long-term consequences. These include:
- The stress and feeling of depression may lead to stomach aches or headaches, excessive weeping or crying, bed-wetting, nightmares, or sleeping difficulties.
- Self-esteem drops, along with the student's self-image.
- Victims may be reluctant to attend school.

Discussion Points

- Brainstorm reasons why people may bully. (Teachers may wish to collate the reasons and discuss after students individually answer Question 1.)
- Brainstorm (or again collate afterwards) words to describe how both people who bully and those who are being bullied may feel. Answers could include:
  – Those who bully – angry, powerful, annoyed, bitter, jealous, envious, happy, satisfied, strong, forceful, in control, popular, etc.
  – Those who are being bullied – worried, scared, nervous, sad, mad, embarrassed, frightened, depressed, etc.

Students will answer differently according to how much, if at all, they are bullied or inclined to bully.

Did You Know?

Student bullies appear to need to feel powerful and in control.

Why Do People Bully? – 1

People who bully do so for a variety of reasons. They may also be unaware of how their bullying makes others feel.

❶ Can you think of any other reasons why people bully? Write them below.

	They may be jealous of the person they are bullying.

They may see it as a way to be popular.	

They may do it because they think they will get bullied themselves if they don't.

They may do it to get attention.	

	They may be getting bullied at home.

They may feel it makes them look tough.	

❷ Make a list of words to describe how a person who bullies and a person being bullied might feel.

angry

scared

How a person bullying might feel

How a person being bullied might feel

❸ In groups, discuss and make a list of tips for people who bully, for example, "Seriously think about what you are doing," or "Your actions could have a serious effect on that person now and in the future." Write on the back of this sheet if you need more space.

_____

_____

_____

_____

Why Do People Bully? – 2

Teacher's Notes

Indicators

- Determines which students in a picture are bullying or promoting bullying.
- Portrays characters in a play to gain an understanding of how they are feeling.
- Decides on the best ending to the play through discussion and acting.

Teacher Information

Sometimes, a circle of friends supports one of their peers who is bullying by smirking, laughing, or joining in. These students are promoting bullying. Other friends may not like what their peer is doing. Instead of trying to stop a friend from bullying, they stay silent. By keeping quiet, those friends are preventing the bullying from stopping. Sometimes, when people don't like what a friend is doing to someone else, they walk away from their friend. They are helping to stop the bullying by not supporting their friend any more. Students who witness bullying may act in the following ways:

- Help the person bullying by joining in.
- Help the person bullying by watching, laughing, or shouting encouragement.
- Remain completely uninvolved.
- Help the person being bullied by telling the person bullying to stop it, by fetching/telling an adult, etc.

Openly discussing ways for students to assist others who are being bullied will help foster an anti-bullying attitude in the school.

Discussion Points

- Which areas in the school are "bullying hot spots"? Map out "bullying hot spots" for your school. These may be areas on school grounds where adults are less likely to be during break times. Hot spots can also occur in the school. Bullying may also occur in the corners of the music/art/assembly room and the classroom.
- Students can discuss the picture in Question 1 in small groups.
- Is anyone in the picture helping to prevent bullying?
- Is the girl looking down promoting bullying?
- What about the boy with his arms folded?
- Think back to a time when you have witnessed bullying in the school. Close your eyes and remember it. Think about which person in the picture represents you. (The students do not need to tell their answers.)

The play
- Why do you think Jerome acts the way he does towards Tiffany?
- Have you ever thought that students who bully may have reasons for their actions other than "just being mean"?
- What kind of support does Jerome need to help him stop?
- How do you think each of the characters is feeling – Tiffany, Jerome, Nicola and Daniel?
- Once the students have completed their plays, discuss the endings chosen by each group. How similar were there? How realistic were they?
- When should teachers/parents be involved in a scenario such as this one?

Did You Know?

Most bullying takes place in or close to school buildings.

Why Do People Bully? – 2

Bullying often happens in front of other people. The person bullying may want others to see his or her actions. Why do you think this is? In your group, think of as many reasons as you can.

❶ Discuss with your group which children in the picture are bullying or promoting bullying.

❷ (a) Read the script below and, in your group, decide who will play each character.

   (b) Rehearse the play, considering your character's body language and expression.

The students are entering the school building, hanging their coats in their lockers.

Nicola: *(walking with Jerome and Dan)* How is your dad doing? Did he get that job in the end?

Jerome: Nah … *(spotting Tiffany)* Hey, Tiffany! Nice bag! That'll look cool on me!

Jerome takes the bag and starts putting it on his back.

Tiffany: *(softly)* Don't Jerome. It's new! Please don't …

Daniel: *(starts laughing)* Heh – it suits you, Jerome!

Jerome: I think I'll just keep it for the day. Look at me and my new backpack!

Tiffany: *(looking down at her shoes)* I'll get into trouble. Please give it back.

Jerome: I can't hear you! Let's go, guys!

Jerome places the backpack high up on top of the lockers where Tiffany can't reach it.

The playground at lunchtime

Nicola: Are you going to give Tiffany her backpack? You are always picking on her and making her cry.

Jerome: She deserves it! She is always showing off her new stuff! This week it's that bag, last week it was her jacket. She's just so spoiled.

Daniel: Yes, but didn't Mr. Wyatt say that you had to leave her alone?

Jerome: I don't know. She's not getting that bag back, though! She can cry all she wants!

Nicola: *(standing up)* Tiffany's nice, Jerome. She can't help it if her parents buy her stuff. I'm going.

Daniel: I think you'd better give the bag back, Jerome, and give Tiffany a break.

Jerome: Whatever!

When I Feel Angry – 1

Teacher's Notes

Indicator

- Identifies the changes that occur to his/her body when angry.
- Recognizes situations that make him/her angry.
- Considers the cause of the incidents and considers a more appropriate way to react.

Teacher Information

Showing anger does not necessarily mean that someone is displaying bullying behavior. It can become this if the behavior is repeated and is physical or verbal to the extreme. Students who bully, however, will more readily adopt aggressive solutions to resolve conflict. They use being angry as a excuse for bullying. Unacceptable ways of expressing anger include hitting and pushing, sulking and crying excessively, or constantly looking for comfort solutions from a teacher or adult.

Most students will become angry at school for these reasons:
- conflict – verbal or physical
- rejection – not being allowed to play with their friends, etc.
- being asked or made to do things they don't want to do
- having their property or space invaded

It is important for teachers to create an atmosphere in their classrooms that allows students to express and manage angry feelings. This can be done by ensuring that all rules are clear, fair and consistent; adopting anger management strategies for certain students (for example, a student is allowed to stand outside the classroom when he/she feels as though he/she is about to explode); good communication; and modeling positive anger management strategies.

Discussion Points

- Is it all right to be angry? What things shouldn't you do when you are angry?
- Is it all right to hurt someone else's feelings when you are angry?
- What signs let us know that we are about to get angry? (Discuss body language, etc.)
- Discuss what can happen to adults (and children) who are unable to control their anger. Sometimes, people do things to property and others when they are angry that are illegal. Explain the importance of learning to control your anger when you are young.
- What could you do to help control the angry feelings you have? What do you do already?
- Ask the students to share the incidents that have made them angry with the class. Discuss their reactions.
- Role-play a situation where anger is building up.

Did You Know?

A child's ability to understand emotions is impaired when he/she witnesses adults showing a lot of anger.

When I Feel Angry – 1

As with other emotions we feel, our body make changes when we feel angry.

1 What happens to you when you get angry?

face: _____

muscles: _____

voice: _____

eyes: _____

other: _____

2 When people get angry easily, they are sometimes said to have a "short fuse." Mark the length of your "fuse" on the fuse scale below.

short fuse

long fuse

EXPLOSIVES

3 List three incidents that have made you angry.

4

Incident	Did you do something to cause this anger?	Was someone else the cause of it?	Can you think of a way you could have avoided this anger?
1			
2			
3			

When I Feel Angry – 2

Teacher's Notes

Indicators

- Lists strategies for dealing with anger and indicates how suitable the strategy is to their own personality.
- Offers anger management suggestions through role-plays or written suggestions.

Teacher Information

As a teacher, help your students to deal with anger in a socially acceptable way. Unacceptable ways of expressing anger include, hitting and pushing, sulking and crying excessively, or constantly looking for comfort solutions from a teacher or adult.

Encourage students to follow the steps they have listed on the worksheet to help them deal with anger. Talking about how they feel and developing an empathy towards others will help them to gain control of their emotions. Teachers can assist by listening and suggesting to the students how to act in different situations where they feel angry.

Ways to control anger include:
- taking a deep breath
- counting to 10
- getting away from the situation or person that is making you angry
- trying to relax your body
- exercising – going for a big run or bouncing a ball, etc.
- trying to stay calm
- thinking and choosing the best way to react
- telling yourself you are all right
- talking about how you feel

Discussion Points

- It isn't wrong to get angry but it is wrong to get angry and take it out on others.
- Think about things you have said and done to others when you have been angry. Have their feelings been hurt? Have they been physically hurt? After an incident such as this, we normally calm down and feel regretful. Have you ever done something to another person that you now regret? Did you apologize?
- Ask the students to share their strategies for anger management. Discuss which techniques are appropriate for the classroom, the playground, at home, etc.
- Look at the list of anger management techniques – which was the most popular choice for the students in the class (receiving the rank "1")?
- How can we help students who are learning to control their anger? (By not provoking them or "cheering them on" when they get angry.)

Did You Know?

Children of bullies often become bullies themselves and will probably continue to bully as adults unless they get help.

When I Feel Angry – 2

We can't always avoid the people or things that make us angry but we can learn to control our anger. Anger is a natural emotion — it is part of life. It is okay to be angry but it is not okay to hurt anyone or damage someone's property because you are angry.

❶ There are many ways to deal with anger. Add some techniques to the list below and score each out of five as to how well the technique would work for you.

❷ Check the techniques you could use at school (S) or home (H).

S	H	Technique	Score out of 5
		Keep a journal or write down the things that make you angry	
		Find a quiet spot to be alone	
		Count to 10	
		Take deep breaths	
		Dance to music	
		Listen to music	
		Talk to someone	
		Exercise – run, walk	
		Talk to yourself "I'm okay," "I'm in control"	
		Tell the person you are angry and why. *"I am feeling angry because ..."*	

❸ Role-play or write how you could help someone else control his/her anger.

(a) Your friend has found out that you and another friend have been to the movies twice without inviting her.

(b) One of the boys in your class is often teased by another group of boys and gets angry each time.

(c) One of the girls in your class always pushes her way angrily to the front of every line.

How Do You Feel?

Teacher's Notes

Indicator

- Considers the feelings of others in bullying situations.

Teacher Information

Role-playing is a good way for students to experience how a person in a situation is feeling. Choose a student to role-play the "victim" in a scenario if he/she normally displays bullying behavior towards others, and vice versa.

Discussion Points

- Students list as many different feelings as they can brainstorm in their groups.
- Collate the feelings on the board and check to see if any more can be added.
- Read the first scenario about Amy, Sarah and Nicola. Sensible children can be chosen to role-play the situation to the class. Write the names "Amy, Sarah and Nicola" on the board. Students choose words that best describe the feelings of each person.
- Repeat for each scenario.

  Scenario 1:

  Amy doesn't like Nicola because she is too "perfect." How do you think Amy feels about herself? If Amy had more self-confidence, would she be worried about Nicola and how much work she is doing? How do you think Sarah feels about Amy choosing her friends? Why doesn't Sarah stick up for Nicola?

  Scenario 2:

  Hacer doesn't like her name because it makes her feel different from the rest of the class. Think of something about you that is quite different from the other people in your class. This makes you interesting and special. Think of things you could say to Hacer to make her feel important and special. Make a list.

  Scenario 3:

  Why did Ronnie feel that he couldn't attend the swimming lessons with his class? What could Brad have said to Ronnie to help him feel better about himself?

  Scenario 4:

  Who should Danny speak to about how he is feeling? (Mr. Shiver, his parents, principal, other students.)

- After reading and discussing the scenarios, talk about the meaning of the word "empathy."

  Empathy: considering other people and their feelings.

  Explain that people who bully others may not be considering how they are affecting others' feelings.

Did You Know?

Most victims will not tell anyone they are being bullied.

How Do You Feel?

1 Discuss, in your group, as many different "feeling" words as you can. Write a list on a separate sheet of paper.

2 Read the scenarios below. List the words that you think best describe how the characters in the stories might be feeling.

Amy **Sarah** **Nicola**	*Amy watched Sarah and Nicola chat together as they walked out of the assembly hall. Amy crossed her arms and frowned, because she had specifically told Sarah that Nicola was "out of the group." During recess, Amy met Sarah in their usual place by the water fountain and said that if she kept talking to Nicola they wouldn't be friends any more. Sarah asked Amy why she didn't like Nicola. Amy replied that Nicola was too perfect and always had her homework in before it was due! The next day, when Nicola walked towards the fountain smiling at Sarah, Sarah walked away quickly to find Amy.*
Hacer, pronounced "Hudge," was always having to correct people in class when they tried to say her name. The girls got it right but the boys would just call her "Fudge," even though they knew it upset her. Hacer didn't like having such a different name, especially because it let people know that she was born in another country. One morning, a substitute teacher was taking attendance, and pronounced Hacer's name "Hay-ser." The boys laughed and started to copy the teacher. Hacer ran from the room, crying and saying that she was going to change her name to Jessica.	**Hacer**
Brad **Ronnie**	*Brad was always telling people that Ronnie was late to school because he was at the bakery, or that his PE top was too tight because Ronnie ate cake all weekend. Every day, Brad made a comment like this in front of a group of children who would chuckle quietly with their eyes diverted from Ronnie's sad face. Whenever the teacher was in the room, Brad would just sit there smiling. During the week of swimming lessons, Ronnie didn't come to school, complaining to his mother that he was sick.*
Danny has always enjoyed school until now. He was a good student who loved being in the top groups for English and math. This year, though, Danny arrived at school late and often went to the sick room during the day with a stomach upset. Mr. Shiver was unlike any teacher Danny had ever had before. Although the tables were arranged in groups, the students were hardly allowed to speak. Whenever Danny spoke, Mr. Shiver growled at him and said that if he spoke again he would have to work through lunch.	**Danny** **Mr. Shiver**

3 On the back of this sheet, describe a situation you have been involved in or witnessed where someone is being bullied. (Use names that won't be recognized.)

List the people in the story and the feelings that they (you) were experiencing at the time.

How Do You React?

Teacher's Notes

Indicator

- Considers personal reactions to scenarios that could lead to bullying situations.

Teacher Information

It is important to address bullying early, as it becomes difficult to break the cycle, for the victim or the bully.

It is imperative that students realize that bullying is not to be tolerated and that they should not put up with it if it is happening to them.

The things that students should not do is:
- Try to keep dealing with the problem themselves – it is all right to ask for help.
- Exaggerate or not tell the true facts. If a part of what they say is shown to be untrue it casts doubt on the whole situation.
- Retaliate by hitting or being verbally abusive. They could be accused of bullying themselves.

Positive steps include:
- If the action is not too serious, just ignoring it or "laughing it off."
- Seeking a peer mediator to help resolve the conflict.
- Being assertive – using "I" statements to express how you are feeling.
- Showing confident body language.
- Avoiding the situation.
- Telling somebody – a friend, adult, teacher, or parent.

Discussion Points

- Which of the scenarios on the worksheet are bullying? Why/Why not?
- Is any one case more extreme than the others?
- There are certain times of the week when we may react in a negative or aggressive manner; for example, Friday afternoons, the day after an evening that involved lots of extracurricular activities and perhaps sleeping over at a friend's house, etc. When are your "grumpy" times during the week?
- Students share their responses to the scenarios on the worksheet with the class if they feel comfortable doing so. Instruct the class that they are not allowed to make any comments if they disagree with the responses.
- After hearing a sample of reactions, discuss which would be the most appropriate and follow the school rules and policies about bullying.
- Who found that his/her partner disagreed with most or every response? Ask the partner to explain his/her reasoning.

Did You Know?

Many adults do not know how to intervene in bullying situations; therefore, bullying is overlooked.

How Do You React?

How we react to a situation can depend on a number of factors. These can include:

- our personalities
- our self-esteem (confidence)
- how we are feeling that day
- if we are worried about something
- if we are hungry or tired

It is important that we think before we react to certain situations.

1 Read the scenarios below. Discuss with a partner how you think you would react. Does your partner agree that you would react that way?

You come to school with a new haircut that you like a lot. You walk into the class proudly and notice that Ms. Laird hasn't arrived yet. It isn't long before the "new haircut" jokes begin. They stop when your teacher enters the room. Halfway through the morning you feel a small bit of eraser hit the back of your neck. You turn around but every one's eyes are diverted to their work. At recess and lunch, the jokes continue. The next morning you walk into the classroom anticipating a comment. You hear a whispered joke and a few chuckles coming from the front of the class.

How would you react?

Does your partner agree? (Y) (N)

You always spend a lot of time on your homework. You make sure that it is well presented and include extra information found on the Internet. Every Thursday, Mr. English discusses the class' homework and mentions any outstanding efforts. Your name is mentioned every week and sometimes your work is shown.

At recess on Thursdays your class is allowed to have the soccer balls. You always try to get one but they are usually all taken. You try to join in with a group that is playing a game but they won't let you.

How would you react?

Does your partner agree? (Y) (N)

Friday morning is the whole-school assembly. Everyone is in a hurry to sit at the back, so it is a challenge getting through the hall without being squashed. Last week, you had been pushed against the wall by Billy and his elbow ended up in your ribs. At the time, you thought it was accident, so you didn't say anything. This week you shuffled through the hall to get to the back of the crowd and, before you knew it, Billy had his elbow in your ribs again.

How would you react?

Does your partner agree? (Y) (N)

Yesterday, you sat with Tayla and Tiffany while you worked on your project for English. The three of you worked well together and sat next to each other at assembly. Today, you hear Tiffany complaining to Tayla that she was sick of you following them around. You went to sit with them to work on your project again and asked if they wanted hang out with you at lunchtime. Tayla and Tiffany shake their heads. Tayla tells you that she and Tiffany are best friends and that you should go and sit with someone else.

How would you react?

Does your partner agree? (Y) (N)

Reacting to Bullying

Teacher's Notes

Indicators

- Identifies positive and negative reactions to being bullied.
- Considers ways to promote positive reactions to being bullied.

Teacher Information

Students don't always react the right way when they are being bullied. Sometimes the person being bullied can not control the situation himself/herself and needs to tell an adult. Many students find this step to be the hardest.

Students may be reluctant to inform their teacher about bullying because they:
- do not want to be labeled as a tattletale
- think it will make it worse
- feel that teachers can't or won't be able to help them

Students must realize that bullying is not to be tolerated and the only way to stop bullying is to be open about it with actions and words. Keeping it a secret from adults they trust gives the person bullying more power to continue. That is why they go to so much trouble to stop the victims from telling.

Discussion Points

- Discuss how everyone has the right to feel safe and that no one deserves to be bullied.
- What is wrong with some things people do to deal with being bullied? Discuss safety.
- Talk about the most positive ways a person could react if he/she is being bullied.
- Should every student who is bullied tell the teacher immediately? Why/Why not?
- What skills could be practiced to help deal with being bullied? ("I" statements, being assertive, etc.)

Did You Know?

Over 70% of teachers say they always intervene in a bullying situation but only 25% of students agree with them!

Reacting to Bullying

1 People react in many different ways when they are experiencing bullying. In your groups, discuss how students respond to being bullied. Record your ideas below.

(lined notebook space for writing)

2 Look at your list. Discuss each type of reaction and decide if it is a positive way to react to bullying or a negative way. Write the reactions in the table below.

Positive ways to react if someone is bullying you.	Negative ways to react if someone is bullying you.

3 Look at your list and consider the questions below.

(a) Which column has the bigger list?

(b) Why do you think this is? _____

_____

(c) Discuss with your group how you could help to promote to other students positive ways to react to bullying. Write your ideas below.

In your classroom: _____

_____

In your school: _____

_____

The Letter

Teacher's Notes

Indicators

- Reads a letter, considering the long-term effects bullying can have.
- Writes a letter in response, expressing feelings and suggesting positive action that can occur in the school.

Teacher's Information

When a person is bullied repeatedly, he/she may feel that he/she doesn't deserve to be treated any differently. This person may lack self-esteem, be overly sensitive and have feelings of insecurity. He/She may also not be as big or strong as the person who is bullying. The latter has a physical and, more importantly, a psychological power. The victims usually behave passively or submissively and do not retaliate when bullied.

Constant bullying can result in short and long-term consequences. These can include:
- stress and feelings of depression which may lead to stomach aches or headaches, excessive weeping or crying, or sleeping difficulties
- self-esteem drops, along with self-image; confidence is lost, mood swings occur
- victims may be reluctant to attend school
- withdrawal from peer group, family members and social gatherings
- learning decreases and work standards drop

It is important to address bullying early, as it becomes difficult to break the cycle, for the victim and the bully.

It is imperative that students realize that bullying is not to be tolerated and that they should not put up with it if it is happening to them.

The things that students should not do is:
- Try to keep dealing with the problem themselves – it is all right to ask for help.
- Exaggerate or not tell the true facts. If a part of what they say is shown to be untrue, it casts doubt upon the whole situation.
- Retaliate by hitting or being verbally abusive. They could end up being accused of bullying themselves.

Discussion Points

- Who has ever had something happen to them that they have continued to think about weeks, months or even years later? This could be a positive or negative experience.
- How do you imagine Alan looked when he was at school? Make a list of adjectives that you think describe Alan's appearance, body language and personality when he was at school.
- What or who could have helped Alan when he was at school? (People – a friend, teacher, adult, parent; Himself – confidence, being assertive, learning about the actions to take to stop the bullying cycle, etc.)
- What could you do if it was your little brother or sister or a friend in Alan's situation today?
- How have things changed to make people more aware of the long-term effects bullying can have on people? (Media, television, criminal acts that have begun with bullying)
- Because we are more aware, does that mean there are no children who feel today like Alan did when he was at school?

Did You Know?

Bullying can have a lifelong effect on a person.

The Letter

To whom it may concern,

My name is Alan and I am 37 years old. I was bullied at school from the ages of eight to 17. (I left school at 17.)

What I remember most about the bullying I endured was not being hit or physically threatened (although that did happen sometimes), but constantly being criticized and made to feel small and weak. I remember feeling pathetic most of the time.

I was never very good at mixing with others and I was quite a nervous child. I always felt that other children found me irritating. I can remember the faces of most of the kids that bullied me on a regular basis. I think now that they were either unhappy, fed-up, or angry (but back then I just thought they were mean!).

Now I wish that I had reacted differently when the kids teased me. If only I hadn't burst into tears and crawled pathetically away every time I was offended or hurt. I can remember clearly when I was in sixth grade, sitting on a bench in the playground, wishing over and over that no one would notice I was there. I realize now that I didn't like myself very much. I should have said, "Alan, you deserve to be treated better than this!" Perhaps then I would have sought help and tried to change my situation.

If my children are ever bullied, I will tell them to take a deep breath, stand up straight and walk away with long confident strides. I will tell them to let the hurtful words "bounce off" their chest and be blown away in the wind, and I will remind them that they deserve to be treated with respect.

Although I still look back on my school days and become angry that I let others make me feel so weak and frightened, I can now say that I do like myself. By having lots of love from family and friends, and by finding out what I am good at, I have been able to feel better about myself.

I hope my letter will be read to children and that it will make them think about their behavior (whether they bully other kids or are being bullied themselves). I hope my letter shows that being bullied can affect a person's whole life.

Yours sincerely,

Alan Littlefield

❶ Read the letter written by Alan Littlefield.

   (a) How does it make you feel?

   (b) Discuss your thoughts about the letter with the people in your group.

❷ Summarize your thoughts about Alan's letter below.

* _____
* _____
* _____
* _____

❸ Write a letter responding to Alan. Include:

   (a) How his letter made you feel.   (b) Any similar experiences you have had.

   (c) The bullying situation in your school.

   (d) Positive actions that you can take to make sure people you know are not affected by bullying the way Alan was.

Conflict

Teacher's Notes

Indicator

- Considers how he/she reacts to being bullied.

Teacher Information

This worksheet does not offer the "perfect" solution to being bullied, as each person and situation is different. Instead, it encourages students to reflect on how they deal with bullying and how they could improve their behavior.

There are, however, some things students should be encouraged to avoid in every situation.
- Students should not try to keep dealing with the problem themselves. Emphasize that it is all right to ask for help.
- Students should not exaggerate or lie about what is happening. If part of what they say is untrue, it casts doubt on the whole situation.
- Students should get away from the bullying situation as soon as possible. Encourage them to find some friends or go to a safe place.
- Students should not retaliate by hitting, etc. They could end up being accused of bullying.

Discussion Points

- What can you do if you are bullied? Discuss some different scenarios and what students could do in each case.
- What might happen if you don't do something about being bullied?
- Discuss tattling. Why is it seen as "uncool" to tell a teacher about bullying? Why is it sometimes important to tell? Discuss how people who bully rely on secrecy.
- What skills could you practice to help you deal with being bullied?
- Discuss things students shouldn't do if they are bullied.
- Discuss the pros and cons of students worksheet answers.

Did You Know?

Four times out of every five, an argument with someone who bullies will wind up as a physical fight.

Conflict

Our reaction to a situation will allow us to decide whether a conflict exists and how big or small it will be. Every person has his/her own style of dealing with conflict.
Read the different styles below.

(a) Work together to find a solution that is good for both people.

(b) Give in to the other person.

(c) Never give in.

(d) Walk away.

(e) Compromise so that both people are partially satisfied.

❶ Which of the styles above would you use in each of these situations?

☐ When you have to deal with someone who is angry.

☐ When you find out you are wrong.

☐ When neither of you will back down.

☐ When the issue is not important.

☐ When the issue is not important to you but is important to the other person.

☐ When you don't have time.

☐ When you have to stand up for your rights.

❷ Below, list some conflicts you have had recently and the style you used to deal with each.

Conflict	Style I used	Style I should have used	Why

Conflict Resolution – 1

Teacher's Notes

Indicator

- Uses conflict resolution skills to suggest solutions to conflict scenarios.

Teacher Information

Students should be encouraged to use discussion to resolve minor conflicts such as name-calling, rumors, taking property without asking, teasing and invading personal space.

Professional peer mediation courses can be valuable in teaching conflict resolution skills. Students are encouraged to attack the problem, rather than the people involved. During discussion, each person involved in the conflict is required to state the problem. Possible solutions are then brainstormed, and a fair solution that suits both parties is reached.

A successful peer mediation program can help to enhance communications and problem-solving skills, create a more comfortable school environment, and encourage tolerance of others. It can also be empowering for students because they are assuming greater responsibility for solving their own problems.

Peer mediation should only be attempted in a school where staff and students have attended a training course. Details of courses in peer mediation can be found on the Internet. Try typing "school mediation courses" into a search engine.

Discussion Points

- Discuss how students usually solve minor conflicts.
- Is there more than one good way to solve a conflict? Discuss the students' worksheet answers.
- What is the value of discussion in solving conflict?
- Discuss how compromise may be needed to resolve a conflict.

Did You Know?

Students who bully become less popular as they grow older, until they are eventually disliked by the majority of students.

Conflict Resolution – 1

1 Write or role-play better endings for each of these scenarios, using conflict resolution skills.

(a) A group of students wants to play touch football on the field right where another group wants to play soccer. A big argument starts and some pushing goes on. A teacher breaks up the argument and both groups are banned from the field for a week.

_____
_____
_____
_____
_____
_____
_____

(b) One student believes another has stolen his wallet and grabs the other student by his shirt and threatens to hurt him if he doesn't give it back. The other student doesn't have the wallet and so can't give it back. The threats to hurt him continue daily.

_____
_____
_____
_____
_____
_____
_____

(c) One student lends another a sweater to wear and it gets torn. The owner of the sweater gets angry and demands that the other student pay for a new one. They argue and are no longer friends.

_____
_____
_____
_____
_____
_____

(d) Two students argue over who will go first in a game. They push each other out of the way and end up in a fight.

_____
_____
_____
_____
_____

2 What did you learn from these situations?

_____
_____

Conflict Resolution – 2

Teacher's Notes

Indicator

- Constructs a board game which reinforces conflict resolution skills.

Teacher Information

Students should be encouraged to use discussion to resolve minor conflicts such as name-calling, rumors, taking property without asking, teasing and invading personal space.

Professional peer mediation courses can be valuable in teaching conflict resolution skills. Students are encouraged to attack the problem, rather than the people involved. During discussion, each person involved in the conflict is required to state the problem. Possible solutions are then brainstormed, and a fair solution that suits both parties is reached.

A successful peer mediation program can help to enhance communications and problem-solving skills, create a more comfortable school environment and encourage tolerance of others. It can also be empowering for students because they are assuming greater responsibility for solving their own problems.

Peer mediation should only be attempted in a school where staff and students have attended a training course. Details of courses in peer mediation can be found on the Internet. Try typing "school mediation courses" into a search engine.

Discussion Points

- Discuss how students usually solve minor conflicts.
- Is there more than one good way to solve a conflict? Discuss the students' worksheet answers.
- What is the value of discussion in solving conflict?
- Discuss how compromise may be needed to resolve a conflict.
- Discuss each of the rules and tips and its importance.

Did You Know?

Boys are more likely to use physical forms of bullying; girls are more likely to use put-downs, spread rumors, practice social exclusion, or use rejection or ostracism.

Conflict Resolution – 2

Task: To construct a board game to help teach and reinforce good conflict resolution skills.

Use all the information below in your board game.

Conflict Resolution Rules and Tips

- *Attack the problem, not the person.*
- *Use "I" statements. "You" statements can make the other person feel defensive.*
- *If both people are too angry it may be necessary to take some time out to cool down.*
- *If you don't feel safe in the situation, walk away.*
- *Respect the other person's feelings.*
- *Listen to what the other person has to say.*
- *Always tell the truth.*
- *Take responsibility for your actions.*
- *Work together to solve the problem.*

Name of board game: _____

The object of the game is to: _____

Board game pieces: _____

Sketch what your board game will look like.

Tolerance

Teacher's Notes

Indicator

- Gains an understanding of the importance of tolerance in the classroom and the community.

Teacher Information

Teaching students tolerance is also teaching them not to hate. Teachers can teach tolerance most effectively by modeling tolerant behavior in the classroom and on the playground.

Discussion Points

- Discuss definitions of tolerant, intolerant, tolerable, tolerate, etc.
- Why is tolerance important? Does it mean you have to agree with other people's beliefs?
- Discuss the outcomes of intolerant behavior in the community.
- What could be achieved through a more tolerant society?
- Brainstorm the names of famous people who have strived for peace through tolerance; e.g., Nelson Mandela, etc.

Did You Know?

Playground statistics have shown that every seven minutes a child is bullied – adult intervention – 4%, peer intervention – 11%, no intervention – 85%.

Tolerance

Tolerance is the ability to accept differences among people.

1 Brainstorm areas of difference among students in your class, e.g., taste in music, size, etc.

2 Choose someone in your class you don't know a lot about. Find five similarities and five differences between that student and yourself.

Similarities	Differences

3 List four problems that may result from intolerance in your school or community. Explain why each problem is important and provide a solution.

Problem	Importance	Solution

Stereotyping

Teacher's Notes

Indicators

- Understands the concept of stereotyping and its possible consequences.
- Practices challenging some common stereotypes.

Teacher Information

We all stereotype people to some extent. However, stereotyping can lead to discrimination and intolerance, as students will begin to understand from the activity.

Teachers can help students by modeling unbiased behavior in the classroom. A good place to start is by avoiding gender stereotypes—many teachers treat boys and girls differently without realizing. Try these suggestions in your classroom.

- Ensure your academic and behavioral expectations are the same for both sexes.
- Use resources that are gender balanced.
- Provide plenty of opportunities for boys and girls to work together.
- Group students by classifications other than sex—even if it's harder!
- Avoid stereotyping classroom chores; e.g., girls cleaning and boys lifting objects.

Note: In Question 1 the nurse is the father of the girl on the stretcher.

Discussion Points

- What is a stereotype?
- Why do people stereotype others? Can it be useful?
- Why should we avoid stereotyping?
- Discuss some common stereotypes and why they might have come about.
- Which stereotypes are the most harmful? Which are least harmful?
- Discuss how students might be stereotyped and their feelings about this.
- Discuss stereotypes in television shows and movies. Why are they used? Which are the most common?

Did You Know?

Physical bullying declines with age, but indirect bullying such as exclusion from groups increases.

Stereotyping

1 *An ambulance arrives at the hospital. The nurse on duty takes one look at the patient on the stretcher, bursts into tears and says, "Oh no! That's my daughter!" The mother of the girl on the stretcher is overseas on vacation — so who is the nurse?*

_____

2 Complete these sentences quickly and then answer the questions below.

All teenagers _____

All elderly people _____

All famous actors _____

All redheads _____

(a) What do all these sentences have in common? _____

_____

(b) Check the responses that are positive and cross out the ones that are negative.

(c) Is the statement true for all people in each group? _____

(d) What is the problem with making statements like this? _____

_____

_____

We often hear stereotypical comments — in fact, we probably make them ourselves without even noticing. The problem with stereotyping is that it can lead to discrimination and intolerance. It also doesn't allow for individual differences. We can reduce the use of stereotypes if we think more about what we are saying or if we politely make others aware of what they are saying.

3 If you heard the following comments how could you challenge them politely?

"Cleaning! That's girls' work."	"Asian kids are good at math."	"All boys like sports."
"I don't agree – my dad does most of the cleaning at home."		

"Scientists are balding men in white coats."	"Children these days have no respect for anyone."	"Kids from that school are smart."

Kindness

Teacher's Notes

Indicators

- Considers the importance of being kind to others.
- Records acts of kindness over a specified time.

Teacher Information

Thinking of and doing acts of kindness helps to promote a positive, caring atmosphere in a school. When kindness is addressed by the whole school, the students will become more aware of others who are not being kind or those who are having unkind words or acts said or done to them. Negative acts such as bullying will be tolerated less as "acts of kindness" become second nature. Focusing on something simple, such as manners, can be a good way to begin acts of kindness in a school. A target such as "Always waiting for someone to walk through a doorway or by saying excuse me if a person is blocking a doorway" can begin a "kindness cycle."

Drama games are a positive and fun way to promote a change in the way people think about and relate to each other. One game that works well is a "circle time" game. The students sit in a circle, one student is chosen by the teacher to sit in the middle. Each student must say something positive about the student in the middle. For example, "He is good at ...," "I like it when she ...," etc. Having the students in a circle is also a good way of opening communication and promoting cooperation in the classroom. Each student can state what his/her goal is going to be for the week to help make the classroom and school a kinder place to be.

Discussion Points

- How does it feel to be kind? To be mean?
- How does it feel when someone is being ... kind to you? ... mean to you?
- How can you be kind to others?
- Do you have to be friendly with everyone? Discuss.
- Discuss how being kind and friendly has a positive effect on both the giver and the receiver.
- If everyone made a better effort to be kind to each other, would bullying exist? Discuss.
- Kindness extends further than just the classroom and the school. Where else can you be kind? (At home, during after-school activities, on weekends, when out at the park, at the mall, etc.)
- Who else can you be kind to other then your peers? Discuss.

Did You Know?

Unless new behaviors are adopted, students who bully will continue to do so. By age 24, up to 60% of children who bully will have at least one criminal conviction.

Kindness

Performing kind acts and receiving kind acts can both make you feel good.

1 Add more kindness acts you could try to the list.

- Invite someone you don't usually eat lunch with to eat lunch with you.

- Write a nice note to someone who seems unhappy.

- Have a chat with someone who seems lonely.

- Invite someone you don't usually play with to play with you.

- _____
  _____

- _____
  _____

- _____
  _____

2 Write an apology to someone you have hurt.

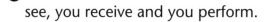

3 Make this week "kindness act" week. Keep a record of kind acts you see, you receive and you perform.

What kind acts did you perform?

What kind acts did you receive?

What kind acts did you see?

"I" Statements

Teacher's Notes

Indicator

- Identifies that "I" statements can be an effective way of coping with being bullied.

Teacher Information

"I" statements are an effective way for students who are experiencing bullying to express themselves to the person bullying them. When students realize that ignoring the bully isn't working, they need to become assertive. Being assertive means to stand up for oneself without becoming aggressive. The bully is also being told that his/her actions will not be tolerated.

"I" statements are likely to be effective because they can not be disputed. Students can begin sentences with "I feel ...," or "I don't like the way ...," so that they can not be argued with because it is how that person is feeling! Also, by expressing how he or she is feeling, the student is not making any judgments about the person bullying them. This way, the person bullying does not feel defensive.

Three points to remember when being assertive and using "I" statements are:
- Begin the sentence with "I."
- State how you feel.
- State the specific behavior you don't like.

Students don't have to stick strictly to a formula as long as the basic structure is kept. For example, "I'm starting to get angry." "I don't like being called names" and "I didn't realize this was so important to you." "Can we work this out?"

Teaching problem-solving strategies through discussion and role-playing will assist students to learn and develop skills for positive social behaviors and relationships. "I" statements are a good example of this. It is also important that the students making the "I" statement have the body language to match. (See page 36.)

Discussion Points

- Explain that the answers to Question 1 are very personal and do not need to be shared with the class.
- "I" statements are a way of expressing your feelings. Why could "I don't like the way you talk to me" be more effective than "You always say horrible things to me. You have to stop"
- Allow the students the opportunity to share their responses to Question 3.
- Role-play a conversation or argument that is full of "you" statements. Ask the class to help change the dialogue to "I" statements.

Did You Know?

8% of students miss one day of school a month to avoid being bullied.

"I" Statements

1 Complete these sentences:

(a) I feel angry when _____

_____

because _____

_____

_____ .

(b) I feel embarrassed when _____

_____

because _____

_____

_____ .

(c) I feel hurt when _____

_____

because _____

_____

_____ .

2 When solving a conflict, using "I" statements instead of "You" statements can be helpful. Why?

_____

_____

_____

_____

_____

_____

Using "I" statements in conflict may feel uncomfortable at first, but they do work and it does get easier.

3 Write "I" statements in response to the following situations:

(a) A girl in your class makes fun of something you are wearing.

_____

_____

(b) A boy in your class makes fun of you because you don't catch well.

_____

_____

(c) A girl in your class spreads rumors about you that aren't true.

_____

_____

(d) A boy in the class starts calling you names when you borrow something of his without asking.

_____

_____

4 Think of a conflict you have witnessed or been part of recently. Write a short dialogue using "I" statements to solve the conflict.

_____

_____

_____

_____

_____

_____

_____

_____

_____

Be Assertive! – 1

Teacher's Notes

Indicators

- Gains an understanding of the way people react to being bullied.
- Identifies how to change behaviors by reading and analyzing a scenario.

Teacher Information

The three main responses to bullying are: being passive, aggressive and assertive. Passive people act as though the rights of others are more important than theirs. Aggressive people act as though their rights are more important than others. Assertive people respect others and themselves equally.

Generally, people who bully are aggressive and those who are bullied are passive. Students can be taught to use defensive strategies to deal with bullying behavior. These strategies can include "self-talk" such as "I" statements and repeating self-affirming statements to oneself. These could include, "I am special," "I deserve to be treated with respect" and "I know the things being said about me aren't true," etc.

Students can also be taught to feel confident by looking confident. Teachers can help by running drama sessions where students participate in exercises where they need to stand confidently, use eye contact and speak clearly. Deep breathing to relax the body can also help.

Discussion Points

- Discuss what kind of attributes assertive, passive and aggressive people may have.
- Can a person be passive and assertive, depending on the situation? Think about the student who is quiet at school but very assertive when surrounded by younger siblings at home. Another student may be very assertive and aggressive on the sports field but passive in the classroom.
- Explain that it is possible for people to practice changing the way they speak ("I" statements) and act (body language) training themselves to be more assertive or less aggressive.
- Show a range of pictures. Discuss whether the person feels good or bad about himself/herself. Students can role-play how they look, act and speak when they are feeling good or bad about themselves.
- Being positive through speech and body language is a good way of attracting friends. People with lots of friends are less likely to be bullied.

Did You Know?

In elementary schools the students who bully are often in the same grade as the victim. The victim is usually younger, if there is an age difference.

Be Assertive! – 1

There are three main ways that people respond to being bullied. These are being:

Passive	Aggressive	Assertive

1 Read the cartoons above. Write a sentence describing three of the ways people can react to being bullied.

Passive: _____

_____

Aggressive: _____

_____

Assertive: _____

_____

2 Read the passage and answer the questions below.

After a few weeks of being bullied by the same girl, Sasha decides it is time to tell her parents. Her Dad asks Sasha how she replies to the teasing. Sasha says that she often replies "You always tease me!" and then walks away. Sometimes she even cries. Sasha's dad takes her to the mirror and tells her to stand up tall and repeat after him, "I don't like what you are saying to me. Stop it now!" He says that it is better to start a sentence with "I" rather than "You...!" Sasha practices her reply and feels much more confident going to school the next day.

(a) "I don't like what you are saying to me." Why do you think Sasha's dad told her to start her sentences with "I"?

_____

_____

(b) Sasha is practicing being assertive (not aggressive). What kind of body language do you recommend for Sasha the next time she replies to the girl teasing her?

_____

_____

(c) Do you think the girl will stop bullying Sasha immediately?

Explain your answer. _____

_____

3 Design a poster that promotes being assertive. Include ideas such as:
- *you deserve to be treated equally*
- *be clear*
- *practice your replies*
- *be precise*
- *respect yourself!*
- *look confident*
- *begin with "I*

  e.g., "I don't ..."
  "I feel ..."
  "I would like ..."

Be Assertive! – 2

Teacher's Notes

Indicators

- Gains an understanding of strategies that help victims to cope with and prevent bullying.
- Chooses the strategy that best suits his/her personality.

Teacher Information

Students can be taught to use defensive strategies to deal with bullying behavior. These strategies can include:

- "Self Talk" and such as "I" statements and repeating self-affirming statements to oneself. These could include, "I am special," "I deserve to be treated with respect" and "I know the things being said about me aren't true," etc.
- Avoiding the situation by staying away from the area where the bullying occurs or by choosing a populated area.
- Using humor can be an effective response to bullying but may not be appropriate for every situation or for every person.
- Being assertive. Students who look unsure of themselves are often targets for bullying. Even using strong words is not effective if the victim's body language shows a lack of confidence. It is important for students to practice looking confident, even if they do not feel that way. Teachers can help by running drama sessions where students participate in exercises where they need to stand confidently, use eye contact and speak clearly. Deep breathing to relax the body can also help.
- Asking for help is essential, especially for victims who are not able to attempt the strategies above or for those who have tried these techniques and they are not working. Some bullying situations can be stopped early on before the bullying cycle begins through peers, teachers, or other adults intervening. Situations where the bullying has been occurring for longer periods may require the victim to practice the strategies above, as well as intervention by a teacher and parent.

Although the bullying may not stop immediately, when a victim uses the strategies above, his or her confidence may grow and perhaps some of the power lost to the person bullying will be returned.

Discussion Points

- Students (who feel comfortable in doing so) can share with the class the strategy that best suits their personality.
- How difficult would it be for a person being bullied to adopt each strategy? Rank them.
- Could a person being bullied adopt all six strategies? Why/Why not?
- How could you help a person being bullied to adopt one or more of the strategies for preventing bullying?

Did You Know?

Body language is an important part of communication. Psychologists say the impact we have on others depends on **what** we say (7%), **how** we say it (38%) and our **body** (nonverbal) language (55%).

Be Assertive! – 2

Each of the stories below describes a student being assertive. They have chosen different approaches to show that they will not accept the behavior of the person bullying them. In their own way, they are showing the person bullying them that they deserve to be treated equally and with respect.

❶ Read the scenarios and discuss them with a partner.

❷ If you were being bullied, which "assertive" strategy would you choose? On the back of this sheet, explain why that strategy would best suit your personality.

Avoid the Situation

Aaron knew that he didn't have a lot of confidence. He was trying to be friendly to the kids at his new school but he wasn't very brave. Whenever he stood near the waste baskets at lunch, two older boys would come up to him and tease him. This had happened three days in a row.

On the fourth day, Aaron moved away from the waste baskets, took a deep breath, and asked a group of boys playing catch if he could join in. They said yes! Aaron noticed that the older boys walked towards the basket that day but left when they saw that he wasn't there.

Use Humor

Some of the girls in Janelle's class called her "Tom," short for "tomboy." Janelle was very talented at sports and always won the shot-put and javelin at field day.

At lunch, one group of girls walked past Janelle, rolling their eyes and flicking their long hair. Although she was hurt, Janelle decided to walk past them as though she was wearing high heels. She flicked her imaginary long hair. The girls rolled around on the grass laughing. Janelle stopped and waited. Once the girls could breathe properly again, they smiled at her.

Tell Someone!

Every Monday, Ahmed, and his friends, Jonah and Eniola, were taken out of their class to have special reading lessons.

As they walked back to class, a few older students working on projects in the art room would try to block Ahmed from getting through. Other kids in class watched and laughed. Ahmed had had enough. He told his teacher, who spoke to the boys' teacher. The next Monday, Ahmed got to his class easily because the group of kids who had blocked him were working on their art project in the classroom by their teacher's desk.

Be Assertive!

Shona didn't know why a couple of the boys in her class enjoyed pushing her and calling her names during break times. Shona had told her teacher, who had tried to help, but the boys only stopped for a few days.

The next time the boys came to her, Shona took a deep breath, stood tall and looked them in the eyes. She said, "I don't like what you are saying to me. It hurts my feelings and I want you to stop."

Own it!

Last year, wearing glasses was cool. Some of the kids would even ask to try them on. This year, the classes were mixed. Billy was always trying to knock Daniel's glasses off or call him unimaginative names like "four eyes."

Daniel liked his glasses. He decided that instead of getting angry or upset, he would just look at Billy and say to him, "I don't care what you say. I like my glasses. They make me look good!." Daniel noticed that some of the girls in Billy's group were nodding in agreement. Billy closed his mouth and walked away.

Tell Yourself You're OK!

Things started to be missing from people's desks just after field day. Nicola and Clare decided that it was Ramah who was taking the pencils and erasers and told the other girls not to talk to her.

Ramah knew that she was innocent. Whenever she heard people whispering about her she would tell herself, "I didn't take anything. I'm OK!" Ramah's teacher praised her for behaving so sensibly. She spoke to the other girls in the class about blaming people without any evidence.

Take Action!

Teacher's Notes

Indicator

- Considers courses of action that could be taken if he or she is being bullied.

Teacher Information

Refer to previous teacher information on pages 42 – 58.

Discussion Points

- Let the students know their Action Plans are confidential. Allow students to complete the worksheet in private if they wish.
- Students who wish to can share their goals with the class.
- How will the students remind themselves about their goals?
- What can our class goal be?
- Could we have a school goal?
- How can we help others to achieve their goals?
- When should we review the actions to see if we are following them?
- Should there be consequences for people who do not follow their action plans?

Did You Know?

When people who bully in elementary school grow up, they will need more government support, have more court convictions, be more likely to be alcoholics, will be more antisocial and need more mental health care.

Take Action!

Many people feel helpless and lost when they are being bullied, but there are some things you can do in any situation.

❶ Complete the action plan, describing the steps you will take if you are being bullied.

Think about steps you could take before telling the teacher, but please ask for help when it is needed.

Sometimes I wish I could stop being mean and have more friends.

My Action Plan   Name: ....

I am going to think positive thoughts.

• I am going to remind myself that I am good at: (⬭)

I am going to tell myself that I have rights and I deserve to be treated with respect.

• My rights include: (⬭)

If I find myself in a bullying situation, I am going to:

☐ stay calm, look confident
☐ keep eye contact
☐ stand up tall, shoulders back
☐ speak clearly, using "I" statements
☐ tell myself that I am not what they say

☐ use humor (carefully)
☐ avoid the person and place
☐ tell someone about what is happening
☐ be assertive!
☐ not be nasty back – it will not make the bullying go away

If I witness bullying happening at school, I am going to:

(⬭)

I am going to help make my classroom and the school be a bully-free place by:

(⬭)

If the bullying continues, I am going to:

(⬭)

❶ Think of a goal for yourself that you can meet in the next week. Examples of goals are:
  • Using five "I" statements during project work in your group.
  • Reminding yourself to stand tall and look confident every day.
  • Doing a kind act each day.
  • Asking someone to play with you who you don't normally play with.

My goal: _____

_____

I am going to practice being more assertive!

Goal Met?   In a week, check if you have met your goal by checking it.

Rights

Teacher's Notes

Indicators

- Devises a list of rights that could be upheld in the classroom.
- Considers any factors that may interfere with these rights.

Teacher Information

It is imperative that students realize that bullying is not to be tolerated. Students have the right to feel safe when they come to school. They also have the right to be treated with respect and kindness, express their feelings and opinions, and work and play in an environment that has consistent, fair rules.

Discussion Points

- Discuss the rights listed on the worksheet. In what countries might these rights not be upheld? Why might this be?
- Discuss that everybody has the right to feel safe and that they deserve not to be bullied. In small groups, construct a list of rights for the classroom. What kinds of things may interfere with these rights? (Remember to stress that names of particular students should not be mentioned in whole-class discussions.)
- Let the students share their ideas with the rest of the class. Choose a few "rights" to copy onto the board. Discuss with the class if there is anything or anyone who may interfere with these rights.
- Allow students the opportunity to share their "classroom rights" with the class if they wish to. Find the answers common to each group.
- How can these rights be adopted into the classroom? What changes will need to be made to address the problems?

Did You Know?

Students seem to give positive attention to the bully rather than the victim.

Rights

The UN Convention on the Rights of the Child set out a list of basic rights that apply to every child in the world. These have been accepted by most countries in the world. The list contains rights such as:

- *Children have the right to an education.*
- *Children have the right to protection from harmful work.*
- *Children have the right to clean food, water and a safe environment to live in.*

This list is set up to ensure countries and their people support the basic rights and freedom of all children.

1 In small groups, develop a list of rights you feel should be upheld in your classroom. These might include things such as the right to be listened to, the right to change your mind, and the right to be treated with respect.

Our Rights	*Problems*

2 In the right-hand column, list any problems that may interfere with the stated right.

Human Rights Heroes

Teacher's Notes

Indicator

- Analyzes and extracts relevant information from an information text about human rights.

Teacher Information

There are many websites that can be viewed to learn more about human rights heroes.

Discussion Points

- How would you feel if you were told where to sit on a bus?
- How would you feel if where you sat depended on your hair color or eye color and that you knew that your hair or eye color was seen as less important than other people's.
- What kind of person was Rosa Parks?
- What else do we know about Martin Luther King, Jr.? What else can we find out?
- Why is it so important that our rights are upheld?
- What can we do if we feel that our rights are being taken for granted or ignored?

Did You Know?

Victims of bullying are more likely to tell parents than teachers.

Human Rights Heroes

People such as Nelson Mandela, Mahatma Gandhi and Martin Luther King, Jr., are peacemakers who fought for freedom and human rights. These people made a big difference to many people's lives in this world.
The following is a description of Martin Luther King, Jr. and Rosa Parks' huge contributions to the fight for civil rights.

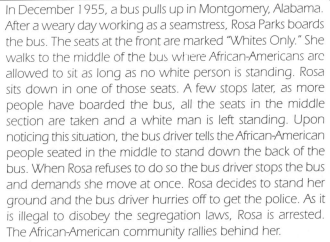

In December 1955, a bus pulls up in Montgomery, Alabama. After a weary day working as a seamstress, Rosa Parks boards the bus. The seats at the front are marked "Whites Only." She walks to the middle of the bus where African-Americans are allowed to sit as long as no white person is standing. Rosa sits down in one of those seats. A few stops later, as more people have boarded the bus, all the seats in the middle section are taken and a white man is left standing. Upon noticing this situation, the bus driver tells the African-American people seated in the middle to stand down the back of the bus. When Rosa refuses to do so the bus driver stops the bus and demands she move at once. Rosa decides to stand her ground and the bus driver hurries off to get the police. As it is illegal to disobey the segregation laws, Rosa is arrested. The African-American community rallies behind her.

A man named Martin Luther King, Jr. is elected to run a large-scale boycott by all African-Americans against the bus company. They decide not to use the buses until the segregation laws are changed. The bus company refuses to change its rules and does not think the boycott will go on. Martin Luther King, Jr. makes a powerful speech to the people on why the boycott must continue and that it must be done peacefully.

"There comes a time," he says, "that people get tired. We are here this evening to say to those who have mistreated us for so long, that we are tired, tired of being segregated and humiliated, tired of being kicked about by the brutal feet of oppression."

The boycott continues, but still the bus company refuses to give in and begins to suffer financially. Shopkeepers also begin losing money because people are shopping closer to home. Things become very unsettled — protesters are hassled and a bomb is set off in Martin Luther King, Jr.'s home. Even after the bomb, Martin Luther King, Jr. urges the people to continue the boycott peacefully—which they do. Nearly a year later the Supreme Court rules the segregation laws are unconstitutional. African-Americans will no longer have to sit in the back of the bus or give up their seats to anyone.

Martin Luther King, Jr. fights ceaselessly for civil rights. Among his tireless actions for the cause, he makes many influential speeches, including "I Have a Dream" and "Let Freedom Ring," which become famous. Many awards are given to him, including the Nobel Peace Prize in 1964.

In 1968 he is assassinated in Memphis. His birthday is celebrated by a national holiday for recognition of his great fight for civil rights.

❶ Why did Rosa Parks refuse to move from her seat on the bus?

_____

_____

_____

❷ How do you know what Rosa Parks was feeling when she was asked to move?

_____

_____

_____

❸ What is a boycott? _____

_____

_____

_____

❹ List three reasons why the boycott was successful.

(i) _____

_____

(ii) _____

_____

(iii) _____

_____

❺ How many years ago were the segregation laws changed?

_____

❻ Discuss why the Montgomery Bus Boycott was such an important event in the fight for civil rights. Record your answer as a class list of reasons.

Consequences

Teacher's Notes

Indicators

- Considers the effects bullying has on people.
- Researches school policies and procedures to deal with bullying behavior.
- Assigns consequences to specific bullying behavior.

Teacher Information

When the students are researching current policies and procedures regarding bullying behavior in the school, help to minimise the disruption by allocating tasks to groups. If possible, photocopy the school policy for bullying and have it available to the students. If there isn't a bullying policy, perhaps ask the principal to speak to the class. The students can take notes.

Speak to lunchtime supervisors about what happens on the playground and to other classroom teachers about their strategies for bullying in their classroom. Define the steps you take to prevent bullying in your classroom.

Discussion Points

- Is there a school bullying policy in this school?
- What steps are taken to stop and prevent bullying:
  - in this classroom?
  - in other classrooms?
  - on the playground?
  - before and after school?
  - in the whole school?
- When should parents be informed/involved?
- Should consequences for certain behaviors be fixed or flexible? What circumstances might cause a consequence to be waived or adapted?
- Who should decide on the consequences of bullying?
- What kinds of behavior will prevent bullying, so that there doesn't need to be a set of consequences?
  - whole-school approach, acts of kindness, setting goals, organized activities at playtimes (less boredom), role-playing and improved social skills, tolerance, improved relationships among teacher, students and parents, etc.

Did You Know?

About 75-80% of students in surveys said they would not join in or would like to help the bullied child.

Consequences

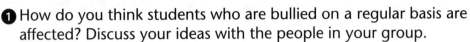

People who bully others need to know their bullying behavior is not allowed and it must stop. They also need to realize that their actions affect people.

1 How do you think students who are bullied on a regular basis are affected? Discuss your ideas with the people in your group.

2 What should the consequences be for a person who bullies?

(a) The following information will help you to consider what happens in your school at the moment, and what can be changed. You will need to speak to teachers, the principal, assistant principal and other adults in the school to find out this information.

(Note: A policy is a document that outlines what should be happening in the school.)

- ❏ school policies about bullying
- ❏ steps taken during break times
- ❏ steps taken before/after school
- ❏ steps taken in your classroom
- ❏ steps taken in the school
- ❏ parental involvement

(b) Write your notes below.

3 List the kinds of behaviors that people who bully display. Next to them, write the consequence that you feel matches the behavior. Continue on the back of this sheet.

Bullying Behavior	Consequences	Will changes need to be made?
		Yes ☐ No ☐
		Yes ☐ No ☐

Notes

Notes

Notes

Notes

Notes